IDENTITY
& GENDER

by

Charlie Ogden

©2017
Book Life
King's Lynn
Norfolk PE30 4LS

ISBN: 978-1-78637-119-5

A catalogue record for this book
is available from the British Library.

Written by:
Charlie Ogden

Edited by:
Grace Jones

Designed by:
Drue Rintoul

Photocredits
Abbreviations: l-left, r-right, b-bottom, t-top, c-centre, m-middle.

Front Cover t – Olga Besnard. Front Cover b – Everett Historical. 2 – Rawpixel.com. 4 – Ollyy. 5 – Eugenio Marongiu. 6 – paul prescott. 7 – conrado. 8 – William Perugini. 9t – Vadim Georgiev. 9b – Alex Brylov. 10 – Yuriy Rudyy. 11 – 501room. 12 – matimix. 13 – Ollyy. 14 – Dmytro Zinkevych. 15 – Brian A Jackson. 16 – lynea. 17l – Andresr. 17r – g-stockstudio. 18 – Rawpixel.com. 19 – anekoho. 20 – Viacheslav Nikolaenko. 21 – oceanfishing. 22 – Everett Historical. 23tr – VSForever. 23m – PHOTOCREO Michal Bednarek. 24 – Everett Collection. 25 – Everett Historical. 26 – szefei. 27 – InesBazdar. 28 – J. Bicking. 29 – everst. 30t – Rawpixel.com. 30ml – Antonio Gravante. 30mr – Dmytro Zinkevych. 30b – Ditty_about_summer. Images are courtesy of Shutterstock.com, unless stated otherwise. With thanks to Getty Images, Thinkstock Photo and iStockphoto.

CONTENTS

Words in **bold** can be found in the glossary on page 31.

WHAT IS IDENTITY?

Every person on the planet has an identity. Identities are the views that people have of themselves; they are the ways that people think about and see themselves. What a person believes and feels strongly about in life can often make up a large part of their identity. This is because people often feel that what they believe in makes up a large part of who they are.

A person's identity is not always something that you can see. In fact, in a lot of cases, a person's identity is only known to them. Identities grow over time and can be shaped by a lot of different things – some that you can control and some that you can't control. There are a lot of different parts to a person's identity, but basically, your identity is the collection of things that make you, you!

Your identity is the view that you have of yourself and it develops over time.

ANIMAL RIGHTS

Many people hold very strong views about animal rights and this can become a part of their identity. People who care about animal rights believe that there should be laws to stop people from mistreating animals. In many places around the world, animals live in terrible conditions – they are kept in very small cages and are sometimes not given enough food or water.

Animal rights **activists** often go to **protests** or write **articles** in order to try to prevent animals around the world from being mistreated. These people have very strong beliefs about animal rights and spend a lot of their time trying to help animals, so these people can often feel that animal rights are a part of their identity.

Animal rights activists often hold protests to raise awareness about the mistreatment of animals.

GROUP IDENTITIES

Sometimes a large group of people can share an identity. When a lot of people gather together to celebrate a belief or a tradition, they could be said to have a group identity.

These people share a group identity as they all follow the Hindu religion.

One of the most common ways that people can share a group identity is through religion. People who follow the same religion could be said to have a group identity, as they share **fundamental** beliefs about the world and how they should live their lives. However, to have a shared identity does not mean that you have the exact same identity as someone else. Everyone's identity is special and **unique** to them. This means that a person can have their own personal identity and share a group identity at the same time.

IDENTITY THROUGH TIME

A person's identity often takes a long time to develop and be fully understood. This is because a person needs to know a lot about themselves before they can really understand their identity and who they are as a person. People often need to have a lot of experiences before they realise what is important to them and what they believe in. Because of this, it can take a long time for a person to understand their identity.

A person's **physical attributes** often have very little to do with their identity. When you become very old, you could look back at a photograph of yourself at the age you are now. Even though you will look very different to the person in the photograph, you will still have the same identity. Your identity will always stay with you even if your appearance changes.

It can sometimes take a very long time to understand your identity, so don't worry if you haven't worked yours out yet!

WHAT SHAPES YOUR IDENTITY?

A person's identity can be shaped by a huge range of different things. Experiences, people, places, conversations and music can all influence someone's identity. Identities are shaped by things you can control, things you can't control and even things that you never come into contact with.

People's identities have been shaped by music for many years.

Knowing what has shaped your identity can be very difficult. However, it is important that people think about what has shaped them as a person as this can help people to understand their identity.

This is because if you know what things in your past have made you into the person you are today, you will know what things in life are most important to you.

PASSIONS

A person's passions are the things that they are most enthusiastic about. Everybody has passions – whether they are games, music, books, countries or animals – and often a person's passions make up a large part of their identity. For example, people who are very passionate about saving the environment will often make this passion a part of their identity.

The things that we are interested in and passionate about can often change as we grow older. This is how your identity can develop and grow over time. As your passions change, certain parts of your identity change as well. However, while certain aspects of your identity will change, grow and develop, many people believe that there is a core part of your identity that will always stay the same. It is this core part of your identity that means that you will always be you, no matter what passions you follow later on in life.

FAMILIES

Members of your family will often have a big influence on your identity. This isn't surprising, as our family members teach us a lot about life and how the world works.

One way that parents and guardians can shape the identities of their children is by helping them to understand what is right and wrong – they help their children to develop a sense of **morality**. Parents and guardians regularly tell their children when they have done something bad and explain to them why it was wrong. People often remember these lessons about what is right and wrong and use them throughout their lives to work out what is right.

Parents and guardians also often pass on their passions to their children - so if cycling is a part of your father's identity, it might become a part of yours too!

CULTURES

Cultures are the ideas, **customs** and behaviours that a particular group of people are used to. Cultures can often involve such things as the food that people eat, the festivals that people celebrate, the languages that people speak and the ways that people act. A person's culture will often come from the country or town where they grew up.

Paper lanterns are an important part of Japanese culture.

People often inherit their cultural identity from their parents. Due to the huge influence that parents often have on their children, children can inherit their parent's cultural identity even if they have never been to the country or town where their cultural identity comes from.

Sharing the same culture is another way in which people can have a group identity. People from the same culture often follow the same religion, celebrate the same festivals and take part in the same **traditions**.

A person's culture usually involves many things that they see as important, which is why culture often becomes a part of a person's identity. When people have a group identity through culture, they are said to have a cultural identity.

11

BEING HAPPY WITH WHO YOU ARE

There are lots of things in life that make people happy, such as tasty food, nice clothes and expensive holidays. However, most people believe that being happy with who you are takes more than just going on holiday. Being happy with who you are involves being happy with the way that you act and the things that you do.

The first step to being happy with who you are is thinking about what is important to you. Once you have worked this out, you can start to live a life that you are happy with. For example, Max knows that the most important thing in his life is football – he can't think of anything he wants more than to be a professional football player. Because of this, a good way for Max to be happy with his life and who he is would be to practise football every day.

Playing football is a good way for Max to be happy with who he is because it helps Max to achieve his dream of becoming a professional football player. Thinking about the future and what you want to become when you get older can help you to be happy with who you are. If someone knows what they want to become when they get older and they spend a lot of their time and effort trying to get to that point, they will often feel much happier with who they are.

But you don't have to think about what you want to be when you grow up to be happy with who you are now! Just think about what you want to be like next year and start working towards that. If you want to be able to play the piano, start practising! If you'd rather be really good at maths, start practising that instead!

A big part of being happy with who you are is knowing what you want and trying your very best to get it.

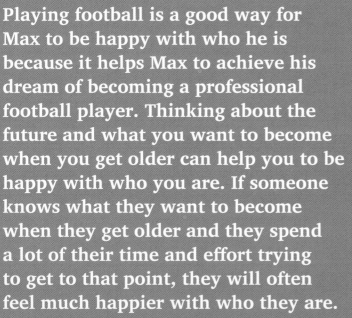

13

VALUES

Living your life according to the values that you believe in is one of the best ways to be happy with who you are. Values are things that people hold very strong views about, just like passions. However, values aren't things that you can see in the world, such as books, games and animals. Instead, a person's values are the types of behaviour that they think are most important, like telling the truth, being kind and showing people **respect**.

Many people believe that being kind and generous are very important values to live by.

A good way to be happy with who you are is to work out the values that are most important to you and to try to put them into practise in your day-to-day life. For example, Imogen might think that it is very important for people to be kind and honest. Because of this, a good way for Imogen to be happy with who she is would be for her to try to be as kind and honest as possible.

ACCEPTING WHO YOU ARE

Understanding that there are things about yourself that you can't change and accepting those things is a very important part of being happy with who you are. There are lots of people in the world who don't like certain things about themselves. For example, lots of people don't like the colour of their hair. Sometimes, when people have things about themselves that they don't like and can't change, they can become very upset.

It is important for people not to hide from the things about themselves that they think make them different. Everyone in the world is unique, so of course people are different from one another! What is important is to learn to love the things that make us different and accept ourselves for who we are.

WHAT IS GENDER?

Gender is often seen as the difference between males and females. This is correct in some situations, however, to fully understand what gender means we have to **contrast** it with 'sex'. 'Sex' is the **biological** difference between the body of a male and the body a female.

'Gender' is the **sociological** difference between males and females, meaning that it is the difference between the way that males and females act and feel about the world. For example, a part of the male gender might be liking spaceships and a part of the female gender might be liking farms and animals.

The ideal image of the female gender in Victorian times was known as the 'Angel in the House'. This term was intended to show that women were supposed to do as they were told and be entirely devoted to their husbands.

For a long time, gender **stereotypes** and gender roles were determined by society and culture. For example, for many years it was assumed that all women would want to have children.

Nowadays, many people are much more relaxed and accepting of others. This has meant that in many places people do not have to worry about their society creating gender stereotypes for them.

The terms 'masculine' and 'feminine' are often used to describe the male gender and the female gender. If something is masculine, then it relates to the male gender and if something is feminine, then it relates to the female gender. When talking about sex, the term 'man' or 'boy' is used to describe the male sex and the term 'woman' or 'girl' is used to describe the female sex – depending on whether the person is a child or an adult.

Woman

Man

From this we can see that gender has nothing to do with our physical attributes or our sex. Instead, gender is determined by each person's individual relationship with the societies and cultures that are important to them. Because of this, there is no reason to think that boys should be masculine or girls should be feminine – be who you want to be!

IDENTITY AND GENDER

Identity and gender are very closely linked and a person's gender often makes up a large part of their identity.

It doesn't matter if you are part of a group identity or not - just be happy with who you are!

Identity isn't usually something that is shown on the outside – for example, you can't usually tell if someone is very passionate about animal rights just by looking at them. However, if someone holds their gender as an important part of their identity, which many people do, you can sometimes notice it. For example, if a person believes that being feminine is an important part of their identity, they might express this by wearing feminine clothing such as dresses. Group identities are also often built around gender. People who feel that masculinity is an important part of their identity sometimes form groups based on this similarity. Other people who are masculine, however, might not be a part of these groups simply because they don't see being masculine as an important part of who they are.

GENDER IDENTITY

Every person on the planet has a 'gender identity'. A person's gender identity is the way that they feel about their own gender and – just like a regular identity – it often involves a lot of their beliefs, values, passions, likes and dislikes. A gender identity is a person's own experience of their gender and the way that they interact with the world.

The Thai flag.

Thailand has one of the most accepting societies in the world in relation to gender identities. Views about masculinity and femininity aren't very strict in the country and people are mostly free to express their gender identity however they please.

For many people, completely understanding their gender identity can be difficult, upsetting and take a very long time. This is because many societies around the world believe that men should be masculine and women should be feminine. However, lots of societies now know that this is not the case and that there is no link between gender and sex. Wherever you live in the world, it is important that you support people who are struggling with their gender identity so that they feel safe, respected and **equal**.

THE GENDER SPECTRUM

For a long time, people thought that a person's gender could be only one of two things – it had to be either masculine or feminine. This is because people still thought that gender was linked to sex, which can only be one of two things – everyone is either a man or a woman. Nowadays, however, many people accept that gender should be thought of as a **spectrum**.

The colour spectrum

To better understand what the gender spectrum means, look at the colour spectrum. At one end of the spectrum there is violet and at the other end there is red. To say that a person's gender is either masculine or feminine is like saying that the only colours are violet and red. As we can see from this colour spectrum, there are many colours between violet and red. In the same way, there are a lot of different possible genders between absolute masculinity and absolute femininity.

The gender spectrum allows for many different expressions of gender to occur in the world, because a person's gender can fall anywhere on the spectrum between masculinity and femininity. This seems to make a lot more sense when you look at actual genders in the world. Many men are masculine, however not all men are as masculine as each other. In the same way, many women are feminine, but not all women are as feminine as each other.

As a person's gender isn't related to their sex, it is possible for a person's gender to fall anywhere on this spectrum. Nowadays, many men consider their gender identity to be more feminine and many women consider their gender identity to be more masculine. These people are known as 'transgender' and the gender spectrum shows that this is possible and perfectly normal.

Rainbow-coloured flags are now used by many people to show their unity with transgender people. They use this flag because of the similarities between the colour spectrum and the gender spectrum. Originally, each colour on the flag was meant to represent a different thing, for example red represented life, green represented nature and turquoise represented art.

21

HISTORY OF GENDER IDENTITY

In the past, people assumed that a person's gender was determined by their sex, meaning that all men had to be masculine and all women had to be feminine. Because of this, men and women throughout history have been **discriminated** against for their gender.

Throughout history, many people have challenged gender roles. One notable person to do this is Amelia Earhart, who, in 1932, was the first woman to fly across the Atlantic Ocean. At the time, most people expected only men to be pilots.

For a very long time, people believed in 'gender roles', which are **traits** that a person is expected to have based on their sex. Men were expected to be fighters and workers, whereas women were expected to be mothers and carers. Throughout history, many people have struggled to always live up to their gender roles. This is because the gender spectrum was not used in these times and people did not realise that not all men are as masculine as each other and that not all women are as feminine as each other.

The way that gender was understood changed in many ways throughout history. In ancient times, in places like ancient Rome and ancient Greece, different genders were believed to possess different kinds of knowledge. This is similar to the way that gender roles were thought about, as the people in ancient Rome and ancient Greece believed that men had knowledge about fighting and crafting, whereas women had knowledge about emotion, care and healing.

THE ANCIENT ROMAN GOD OF LOVE, CUPID, WAS OCCASIONALLY DEPICTED AS BEING TRANSGENDER. THIS REVEALS THAT SOME ANCIENT SOCIETIES ACCEPTED PEOPLE REGARDLESS OF THEIR GENDER IDENTITY.

However, transgender people in these ancient societies were not discriminated against like they were in other parts of history. Instead, transgender people were seen to possess both the masculine and the feminine sides of knowledge. Because of this, transgender people were often well respected in ancient Rome and ancient Greece.

In more recent history, transgender people were commonly discriminated against by their community. Many of the **civilisations** that became powerful throughout history thought that men were better than women, which led to a lot of people being discriminated against for their sex and gender. In these societies, women were always worse off than men, no matter what their gender identity was. As well as this, men were often only respected if they had a masculine gender identity, meaning that many men were discriminated against because they had gender identities that weren't considered to be masculine enough.

Gender-based discrimination occurred in almost every war in history. Women were often not allowed to be soldiers in wars as fighting was seen as a man's duty. On top of this, many men who did not want to fight were discriminated against for not being masculine enough.

Unfortunately, it is difficult to know exactly how communities treated transgender people in the distant past as there were very few records kept about them. However, this isn't because there were no transgender people back then. Instead, it is likely that people were often afraid to express their gender because they were scared that they might be discriminated against.

OSCAR WILDE, A FAMOUS VICTORIAN PLAYWRIGHT, POET AND AUTHOR, WAS ONE OF THE FIRST CELEBRITIES TO CHALLENGE SOCIAL VIEWS ABOUT GENDER IN HIS WORK AND IN REAL LIFE.

Many societies started to become safer and more accepting places in the 1900s. Because of this, the number of people who identified as transgender grew very quickly. While people were still often discriminated against for their gender identity, the idea that men could be feminine and women could be masculine started to become accepted. This led to many transgender people being more open about their identity.

GENDER TODAY

Governments from all around the world have passed laws to try to give people of any gender equal rights, equal opportunities and an equal status in their societies. In the UK, it is now illegal for someone to be refused a job or an education based on their gender identity. On top of this, people of any gender are allowed to marry each other. In 2004, the UK government also passed the Gender Recognition Act, which made it legal for someone to change their sex if they felt that it better suited their gender identity.

In recent years, lots of people have joined the gender neutrality movement. This is the idea that laws and language should avoid distinguishing between different genders as this promotes the old belief that there are only two genders, rather than a spectrum.

The Indian flag.

Many other governments have also made laws that try to make transgender people feel more welcome and at home in their own country. One of these countries is India, which, in 2014, made 'transgender' the country's third official gender.

The Indian government did this because they believed that a person's gender identity is a core part of their right to freedom, meaning that people should always feel free to express their gender, no matter where their gender falls on the gender spectrum.

It is important for everyone in today's society to respect and accept people no matter what their gender identity is. Understanding your gender identity can take a very long time and sometimes people can become very frustrated by it. Often transgender people are worried that their families and friends might not accept their gender identity. It is important to always treat people equally, no matter what their gender identity is, so that they can feel comfortable and welcome in their community.

If you are having trouble understanding your gender identity, it can sometimes help to talk about it with someone. When you're with someone that you know and trust, talk to them about your gender identity and how it makes you feel. It is important to understand that your gender identity is normal and natural, no matter where it falls on the gender spectrum.

CHARITIES

There are many groups of people around the world who try to improve social rights for transgender people and help to prevent transgender people from being discriminated against. One organisation in the UK that is well known for doing this is called Press For Change. The people in this group try to make it so that all transgender people in the UK are respected and treated equally by their community.

These people gathered in North Carolina, U.S.A. in order to protest for the rights of transgender people.

Press For Change were one of the main **charities** to promote human rights for transgender people in the UK in the 1990s. Human rights are actions that all people should be allowed to perform simply because they are human. This means that everyone has human rights, no matter what their gender is. Over the last 30 years, many organisations and charities, including Press For Change, have tried to protect the human rights of transgender people. One of the most common ways that charities do this is by gathering at protests, as this helps to raise awareness about transgender issues and shows people that the human rights of transgender people need to be protected.

Other charities and organisations around the world try to help by changing the way that societies view transgender people. Unfortunately, there are some people who find it difficult to understand what it means to be transgender. This can lead to discrimination towards those who identify themselves as transgender. Many organisations around the globe are trying to prevent this kind of behaviour from happening by teaching people about what it means to be transgender. While there are still cases where transgender people are not treated the same as others, the world is becoming a more diverse, accepting and tolerant place all the time. It is extremely important to be accepting of others, regardless of their gender identity, so that no one is afraid to be open with their gender identity.

ACTIVITY

Can you think of anything that has shaped your identity?
Use the pictures below for ideas!

GLOSSARY

activists	people who try to make social change by doing things like holding protests
articles	pieces of writing that are included alongside others in a newspaper or a magazine
biological	relating to the body and how it works
charities	organisations that try to help people and don't make any profit
civilisations	the societies, cultures and ways of life of certain areas
contrast	to show how one thing is different from another thing
customs	traditional and widely accepted ways of behaving or doing things that are specific to a particular society, place, or time
discriminated	someone who has been treated differently because of their race, gender, religion, sex or age
equal	to be the same as
fundamental	something that is core or of central importance
morality	a person's sense of what is right and what is wrong
physical attributes	the features of your body, such as your height and the colour of your hair
protests	actions that express a disapproval of something, usually involving multiple people
respect	to consider the feelings, wishes and rights of other people
sociological	relating to society and human behaviour
spectrum	a scale with extremes at each end
stereotypes	assumptions that are made about a person because of their gender, sex, religion or nationality
traditions	beliefs or ways of doing things that have been passed down from one generation to the next
traits	a quality or characteristic of a person
unique	being the only one of its kind

INDEX